How to Make Masks

Table of Contents

History of Masks...2
Materials..3
Marking the Eyes..4
Hair...5
Paper Bag Mask..6
Paper Bag Half-Mask..7
Paper Bag Dragon...8
Construction Paper Masks...9
Construction Paper Shield Mask...10
Picnic Plate and Cup Mask..11
Cylinder Mask..12
Totem Pole "Masks"..13
Totem Patterns..14
Half-Mask Patterns..15
Sculptured Aluminum Foil..17
Drinking Straw Mask...18
3-D Bird Beak and Feathers Patterns...19
3-D Eyes, Lashes and Brows Patterns...20
3-D Mouths Patterns...21
3-D Nose and Ear Patterns..22
Clown Mask...23
Eskimo Mask to Color...24
Mexican Mask to Color...25
Ceylonese Mask to Color...26
American Indian Mask to Color...27
Chinese Mask to Color...28
Japanese Mask to Color..29
African Mask to Color...30
Greek Mask to Color..31
Reading List..32

© 1988 by EVAN-MOOR CORP.

History of Masks

Since the beginning of time, masks have been used to represent the forces of nature: sun, moon, rain, wind, etc. Masks were also used to represent the forces of human nature. Masks have been used in every corner and in every culture of the world.

The Eskimos believed that they could change into an animal or a human whenever they wished. This duality provided a perfect outlet for masks. They created ceremonial masks of both human and animal form, all in one.

The American Indians used masks to mourn their dead. They would wear a mask representing the person who died. They also used masks to call on the forces of nature. For example, if they needed rain, they would wear a mask made especially to be worn while they did a rain dance.

The masks of Asia often depict human emotions: anger, humor, fear, joy and grief.

In Japan, the famous Noh masks are considered to be some of the world's most beautiful. Actors, with the help of masks, told the stories of their ancient Gods and their victorious battles over evil demons.

In Greek and Roman times, masks were used most often in the theater. Masks made it possible for one actor to play many roles. An actor could be young one minute and old the next.

The masks of the 15th century Italian theater troupe, commedia dell'arte represented characters still seen today, such as Harlequin the clown.

The giant dragon that the Chinese parade through the streets every year to celebrate the new year is actually a giant mask. Mardi Gras is another place where we see giant masks paraded through the city streets.

Clowns in the circus put on a type of mask each time they paint their faces. No costume was complete for a masquerade ball without the mask, often ornate, usually carried on a stick.

Children at Halloween still carry on the tradition of wearing masks.

The mask at its best is a personal creation of the wearer, crafted by his own hands.

Materials

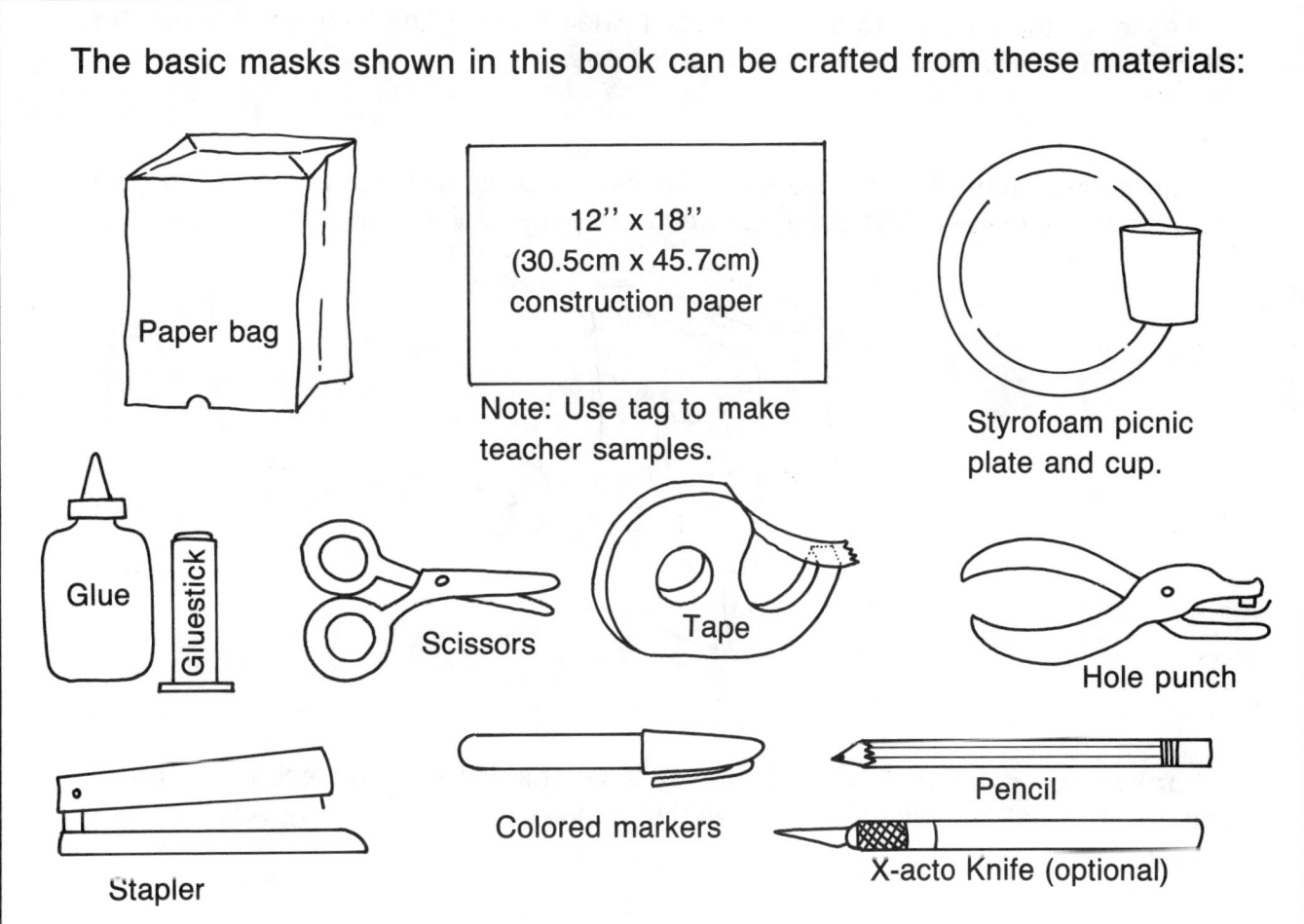

The basic masks shown in this book can be crafted from these materials:

Paper bag

12" x 18" (30.5cm x 45.7cm) construction paper

Note: Use tag to make teacher samples.

Styrofoam picnic plate and cup.

Glue, Gluestick, Scissors, Tape, Hole punch

Stapler, Colored markers, Pencil, X-acto Knife (optional)

The following is a list of materials you can consider for decorating your basic mask:

- Yarn/roving/raffia
- Scraps of construction paper
- Pipe cleaners
- Egg cartons
- Toothpicks
- Beans
- Straws
- Fabric Scraps
- Colored aquarium gravel
- Buttons
- Spaghetti/noodles
- Artificial flowers
- Cotton Balls
- Ribbon
- Cereal, oatmeal, Cheerios
- Styrofoam or paper cups
- Aluminum foil
- Tissue paper
- Paper clips
- Toilet paper rolls
- Felt
- Glitter
- Contact paper
- Feathers

NOTE: Anything that will receive glue, and is small enough, becomes material acceptable for mask decorating.

© 1988 by EVAN-MOOR CORP.

Marking the Eyes

Please tell the children to be very careful when marking the location of their eyes. **NEVER USE A PENCIL POINT** poked at the eye.

The safest method is to have them dip their fingertip in water and press in gently. The water will make a little damp spot and the paper will wrinkle slightly.

For heavier materials (tag for example), have children mark a piece of writing paper with a wet fingertip. Using the writing paper as a template they can then mark the tag.

Construction paper and tag masks are placed over the eyes, unlike the bag mask that rests on the top of the head. If a child places the eye holes too high or too low it won't really matter, however...

The Paper Bag Mask sits on the top of the head so the eyes will have to be marked in the right spot.

"**The eyes are all wrong, I'll have to start over.**" Maybe not, as you can always cut the holes a little bigger, or a lot bigger.

Hair

The whole paper bag, or the paper bag cut into the half-mask, can easily be fringed to create hair. Roll some or all of the fringe pieces around a pencil (see inset) to help them curl.

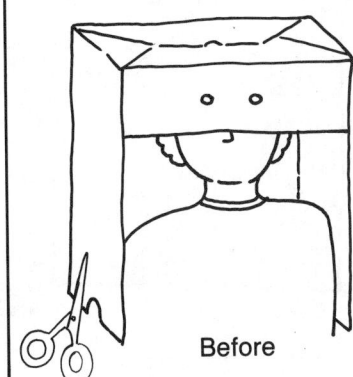
Before

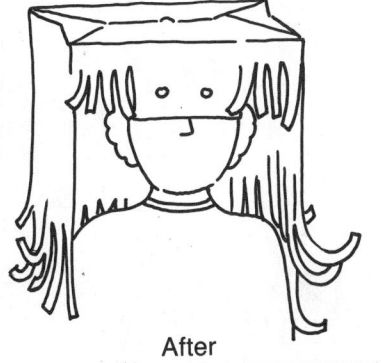
After

or —

The suggestions shown on this page will help you with some basic ideas. Don't limit yourself to these.

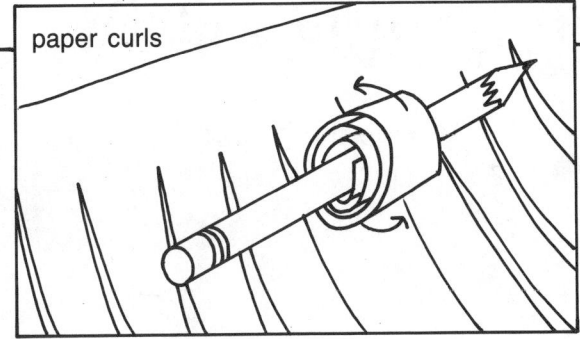
paper curls

Materials that lend themselves to hair:
- yarn/roving/raffia
- paper
- cotton balls
- tissue paper
- oatmeal

Glue cotton balls to the mask for white hair.

Use yarn, roving or raffia to make braids and bangs.

Begin with three clumps of roving held at the top with a rubber band.

Crumpled paper: use different colors for a wonderful effect.

Draw a beard on construction paper. Cut out and glue to mask.

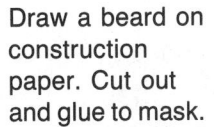
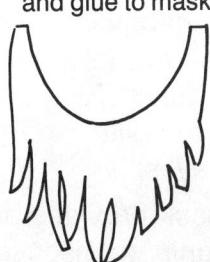

Mustache is a short strip of construction paper, fringed on ends only.

Make lots of paper curls, (see inset) and glue to mask.

Paper Bag Mask

 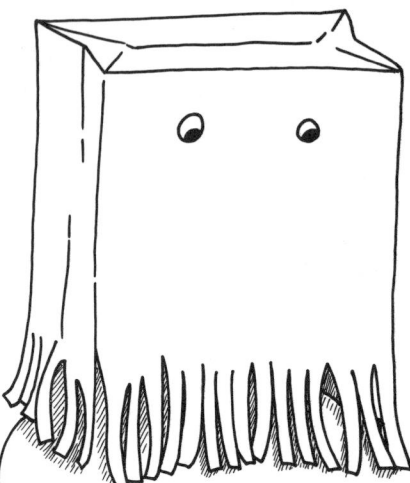 

Mark the location of the eyes (see pg. 4). Cut eye holes.

Cut on folds as shown so bag can rest on head.

Fringe the bottom or...

Roll-up to form collar.

Then...

Add cut-out features from patterns on pgs. 20-22 in this book, or create your own. Glue features to bag.

Or...

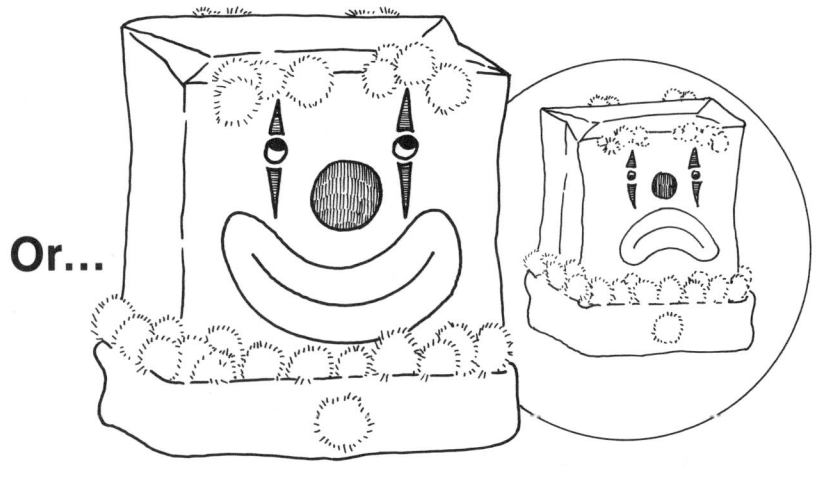

Have children cut eye holes on both sides of paper bag. Draw a happy clown on one side and an unhappy clown on the other. Tuck cotton balls into collar, and glue above eyes.

This mask provides an opportunity to discuss feelings.

© 1988 by EVAN-MOOR CORP.

Paper Bag Half-Mask

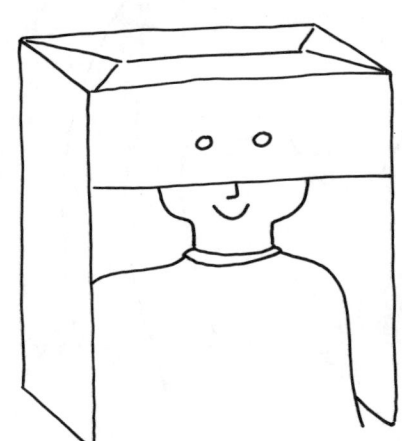

Remove most of one side of bag.

Glue on some feathers cut from a variety of colors (see feather pattern on page 19). Add a nose or a beak (pages 19 and 22) to create a beautiful exotic bird.

Scales for Paper Bag Dragon on page 8.

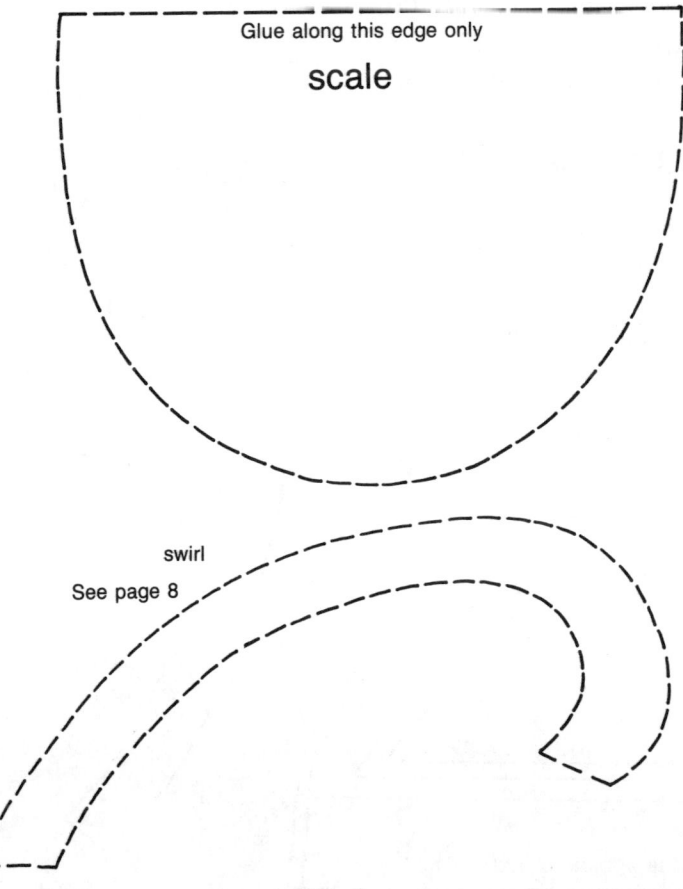

Glue along this edge only

scale

swirl
See page 8

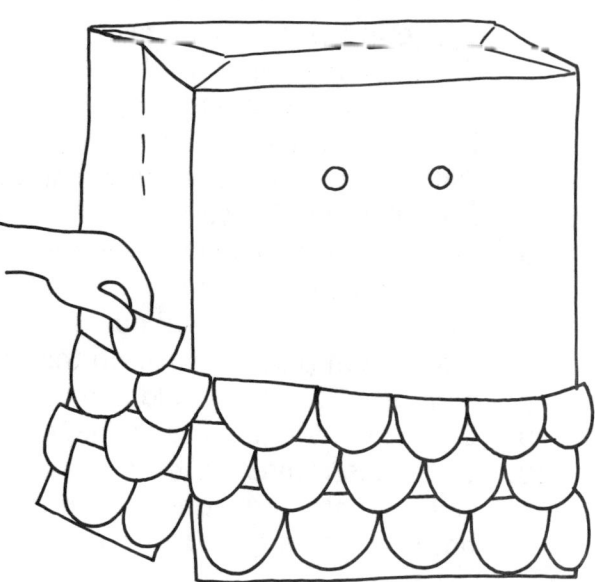

Always begin layering the scales at the bottom. Offset each row, and remember to overlap. Older children can create patterns by using different color scales.
Glue along the top of the scale.
Note: The more you overlap, the more rows you will need.

Paper Bag Dragon

Begin with one large brown grocery bag.

Note: This mask will work as well with only a few rows of scales.

Create this dragon along with a study of Chinese New Year.

1. Cut eye holes in bag. Cover bottom of bag with scales. (See page 7.)
2. Glue 3 circles, in different colors, over eyes. Be sure to cut a hole in the center of each circle before you glue in place.
3. Cut as many paper swirls as you like (pattern on this page). Use these pattern pieces, or create your own swirls.
4. Glue as many eyebrow swirls in place as you wish.
5. Cut two spirals out of red construction paper for nostrils. Glue the ends only.
6. Add orange and yellow swirls for flames out of nostrils.
7. Cut a zig-zag row of teeth out of white paper. Glue in place. Lift teeth to stick out.
8. Use mouth pattern piece on this page. Color mouth with markers. Fold along fold line and glue over teeth.
9. Cut a pink tongue in any shape and glue under teeth.
10. Cover the remainder of the bag with scales if you wish.
11. Cut long strips of construction paper (1" wide) and glue to back to act as tail. Or... you can cover a tail with scales.

Tie ribbons to a stick or tongue depressor to carry when wearing mask.

Glue along this edge, fold under on fold line, glue to bag.

© 1988 by EVAN-MOOR CORP.

Construction Paper Masks

Note: Make these basic shapes out of tag to keep in a center. Children can refer to them when making their own.

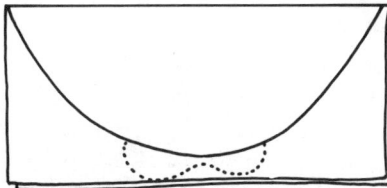

1. Fold construction paper in half, lengthwise.
2. Draw half-circle, or oval, on the folded edge. Cut out circle (or oval). Older children may want to add an ear to the half-circle (shown with dotted line).

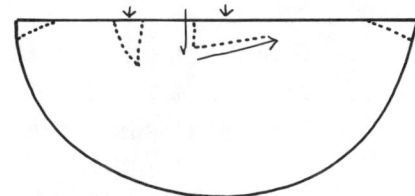

3. Cut little pie shapes out of the corners.
4. Cut a nose in the center. Snip in about 1'', then up about 2'', cutting back toward the fold. If you are using your mask for a drama, cut mouth at this time as well.
5. Mark the eyes. (See page 4.) Cut eye holes.
6. Open up your mask. It will look like this:

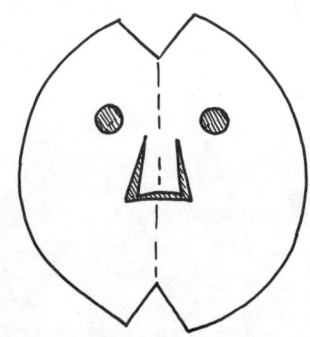

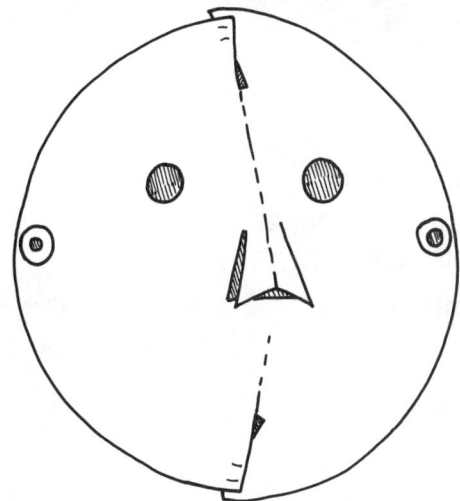

7. Overlap the pie cut and staple. Now your mask has a dimensional shape.
   Put reinforcements over holes, front and back.

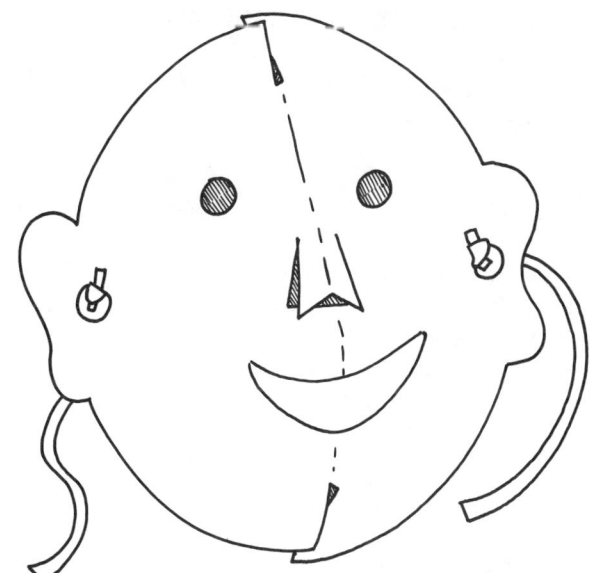

8. The same mask shown with the mouth and ears added. You will need to fold ears forward slightly to help them stick out.

Tie a knot in the ends of two pieces of ribbon or roving. Thread through holes.

© 1988 by EVAN-MOOR CORP.

Construction Paper Shield Mask

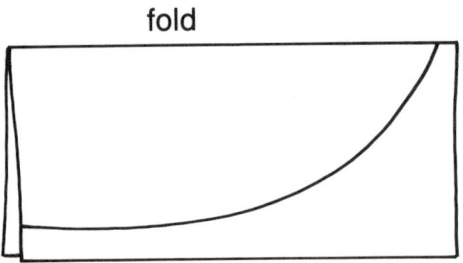

fold

1. Fold construction paper in half, lengthwise.
2. Draw a line as shown above.

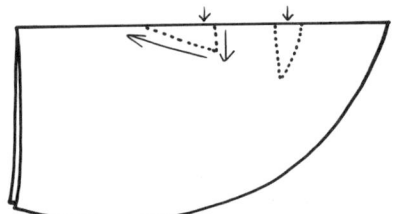

3. Cut out the shield. Cut a nose. Cut into the fold about 1'', then up about 2'', cutting back toward the fold.
4. If you wish to add a mouth, do so now.

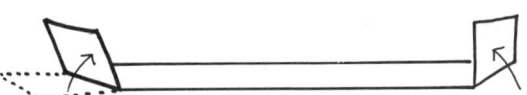

6. Cut a strip of construction paper (or tag) approximately 1'' x 10.'' Fold the ends up on an angle.

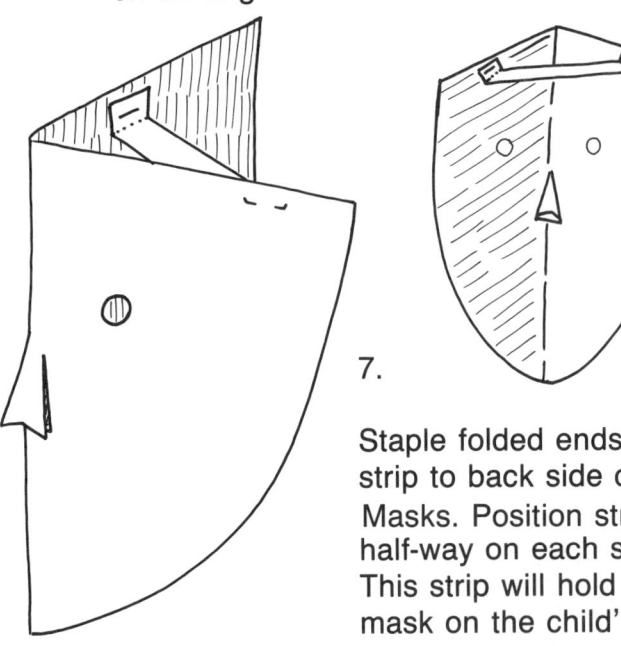

7. Staple folded ends of strip to back side of Masks. Position strip about half-way on each side. This strip will hold the mask on the child's head.

8. Have child place mask on head and mark eye positions. Cut holes.

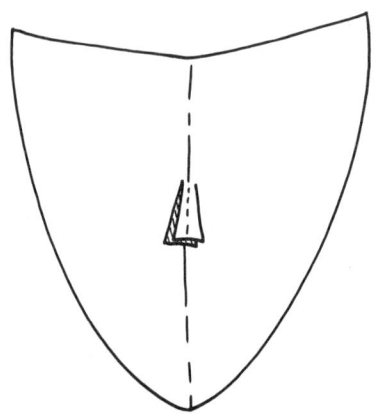

5. Open up your mask. It will look like this.

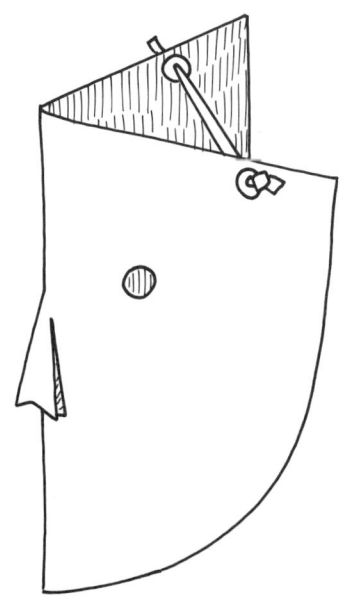

Another way of creating the head rest is with a string.
Punch holes and cover with reinforcements. Knot one end of string or roving. Pull through both holes. Position on child's head and tie knot in other end.

© 1988 by EVAN-MOOR CORP.

Picnic Plate and Cup Mask

This mask is very simple to make. The easiest material to work with is Styrofoam. Use a feather pattern on page 19 to create Kachina Mask on page 27.

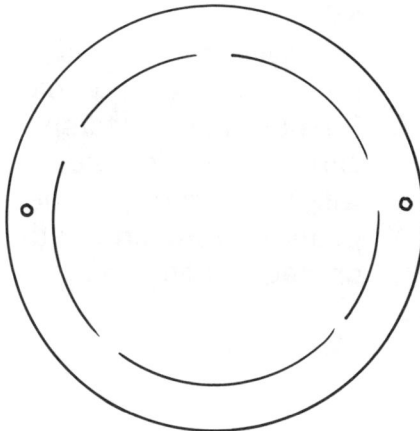

1. Punch holes on sides of plate.

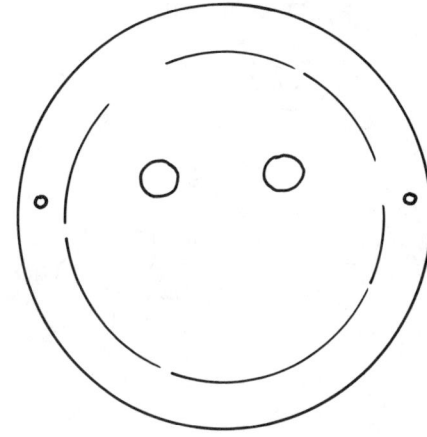

2. Cut holes for eyes. You will need to help children with this step as the material is rigid.

3. Cut straight down into cup, about ¾".

4. Cut off entire top of cup, then cut ring in half.

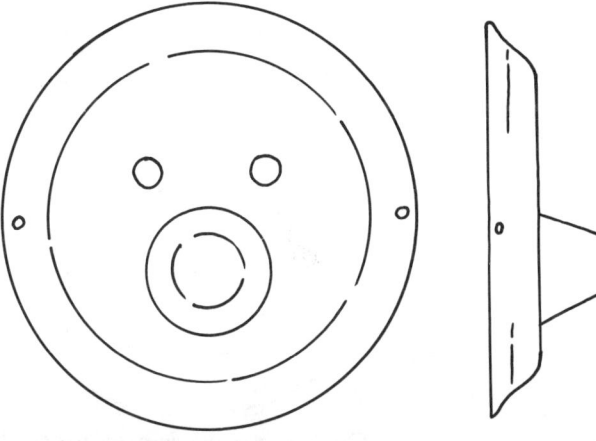

5. Glue bottom edge of cup to plate to form nose. (This makes a great pig snout.)

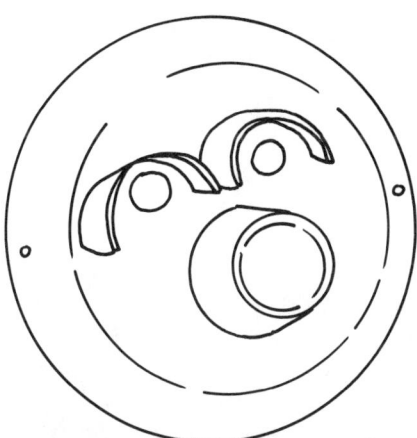
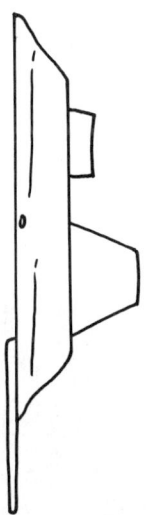

6. Glue two cup ring halves over eyes. Thread string or ribbon through holes.
You can also glue a tongue depressor to the lower rim and use as a hand-held mask.

© 1988 by EVAN-MOOR CORP. Masks

Cylinder Mask

Children design and decorate the cylinder mask flat. Instruct them to use lightweight materials. When the cylinder is wrapped around their head it will rest on their shoulders.

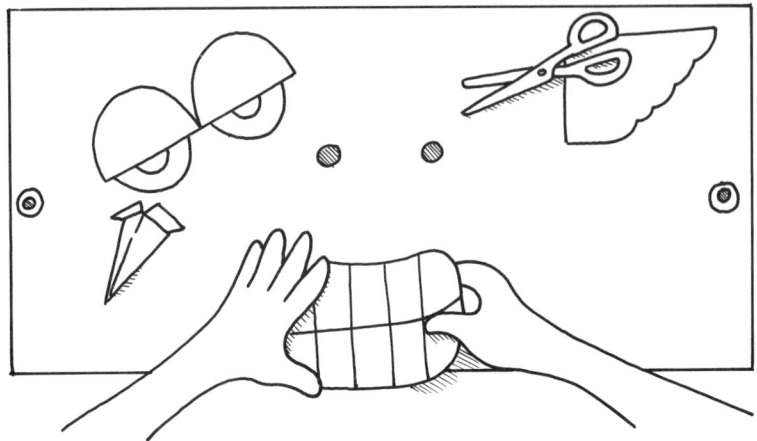

NOTE:
The cylinder shape is perfect for creating Totem Pole designs. Children can draw the features on with markers or use the pattern pieces provided on pages 12-14.

Have children use a writing-paper template to locate eye positions (see page 4). Cut eye holes. Punch holes for ribbon or string ties. Cover holes with reinforcements.

Children create the mask flat then tie it around their heads.

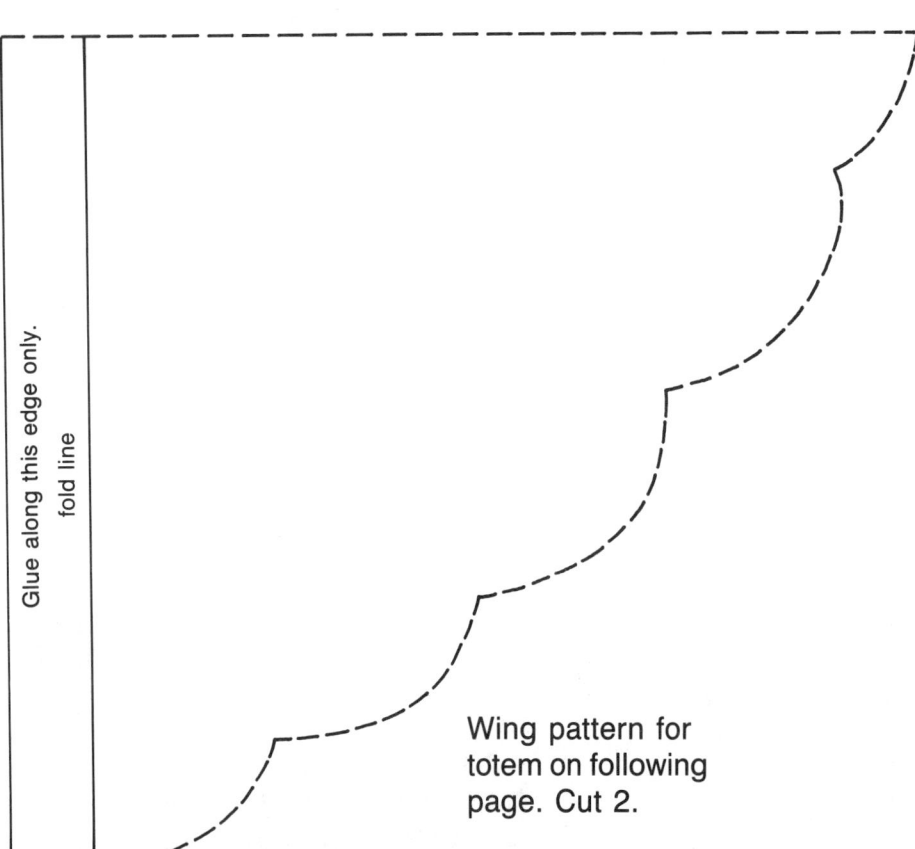

Glue along this edge only.
fold line

Wing pattern for totem on following page. Cut 2.

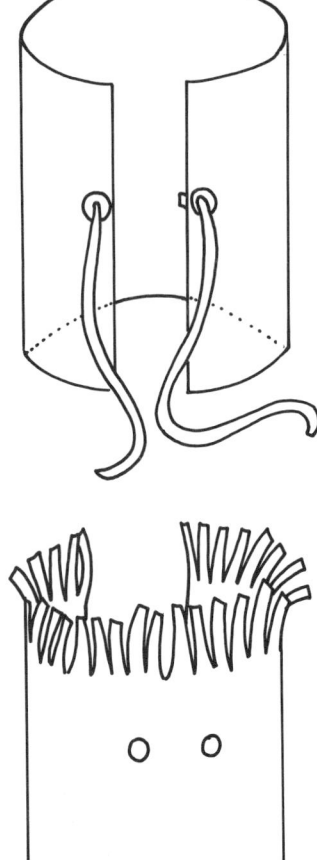

Children can fringe just the top 2 or 3 inches to create hair. If you're creating a totem, the fringed one must be on the top.

© 1988 by EVAN-MOOR CORP.

Totem Pole "Masks"

Children can work on individual sections of the totem. When the parts are complete, staple two together, then roll in a cylinder shape and staple again. This step requires more than two hands. Don't try to put more than three together.

There is no need to cut eyeholes if children don't plan to wear them.

There is no special order; mix and match mouths, noses and eyes as you wish.

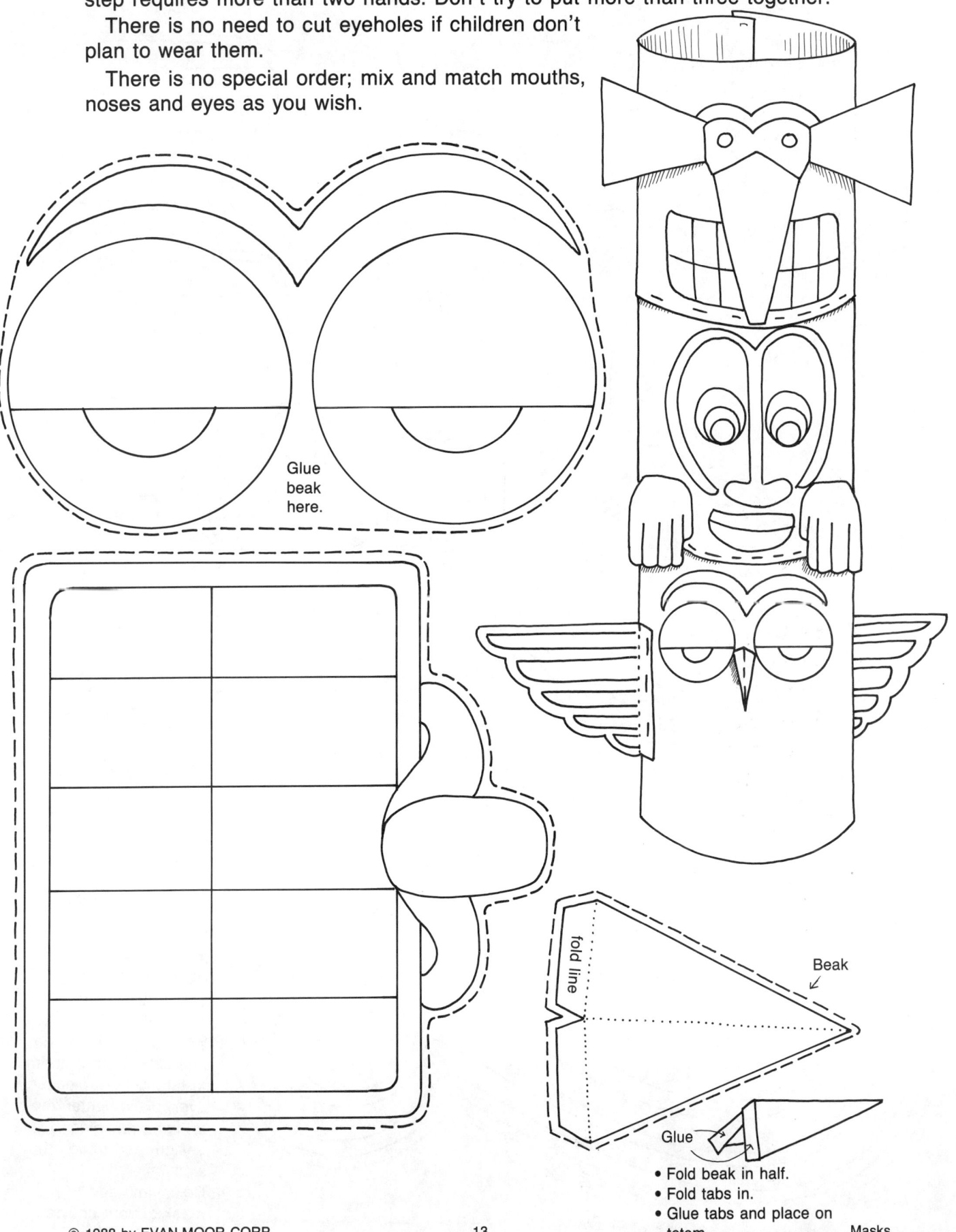

Glue beak here.

fold line

Beak

Glue

- Fold beak in half.
- Fold tabs in.
- Glue tabs and place on totem.

© 1988 by EVAN-MOOR CORP.

Masks

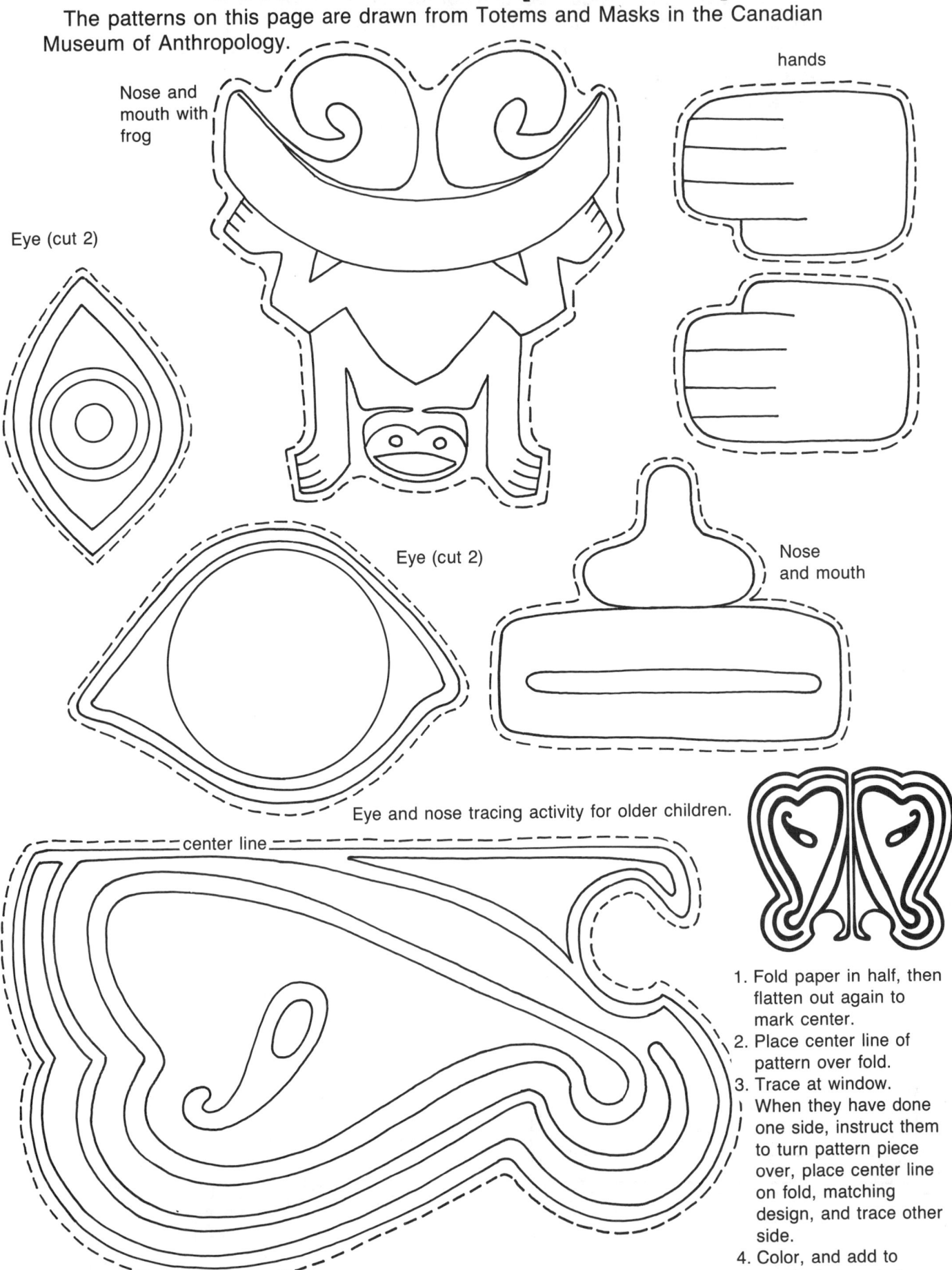

Half-Mask Patterns

Make tag templates from the patterns on pages 15 and 16. Have children fold a piece of construction paper in half and trace the half-mask pattern on the construction paper.

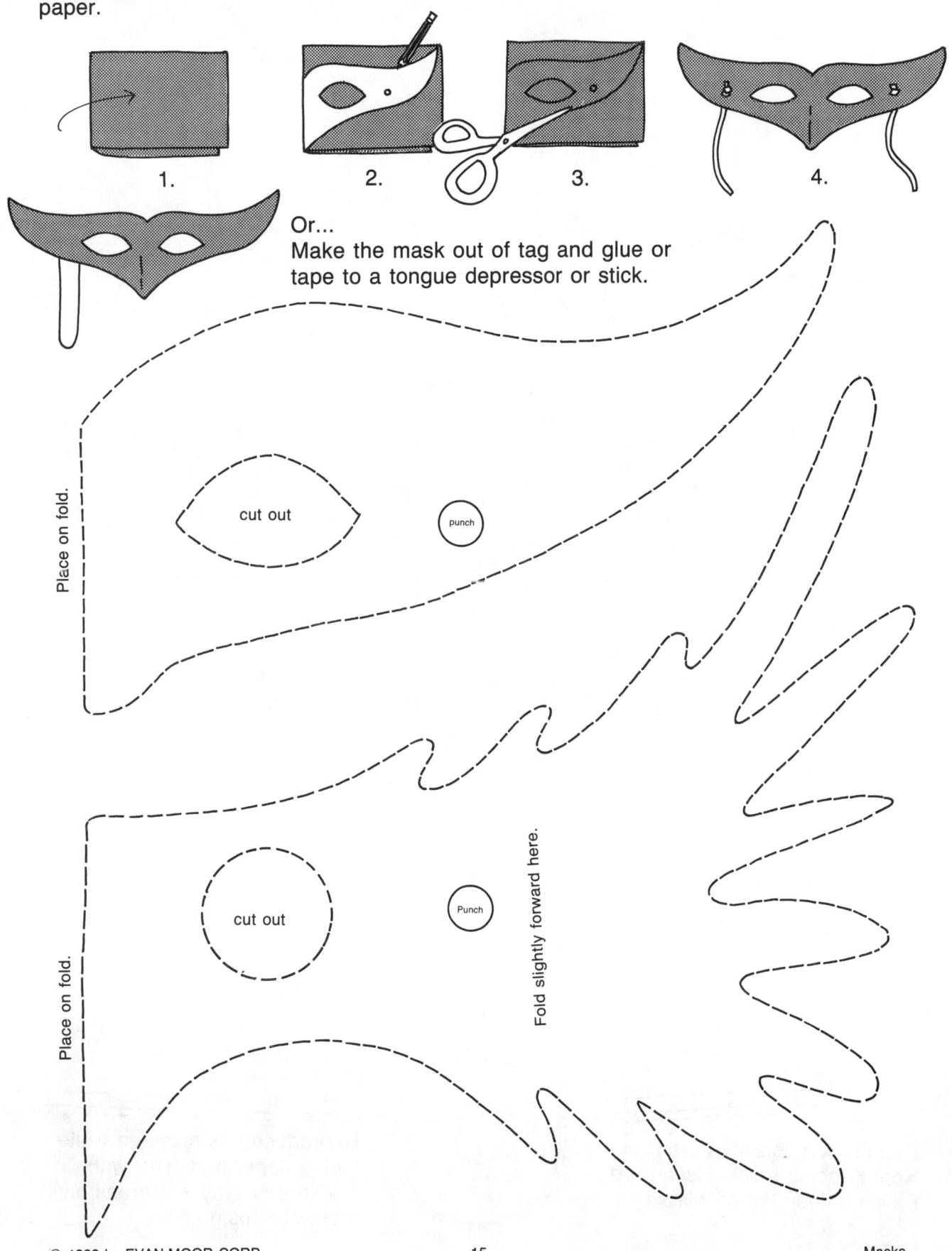

Or...
Make the mask out of tag and glue or tape to a tongue depressor or stick.

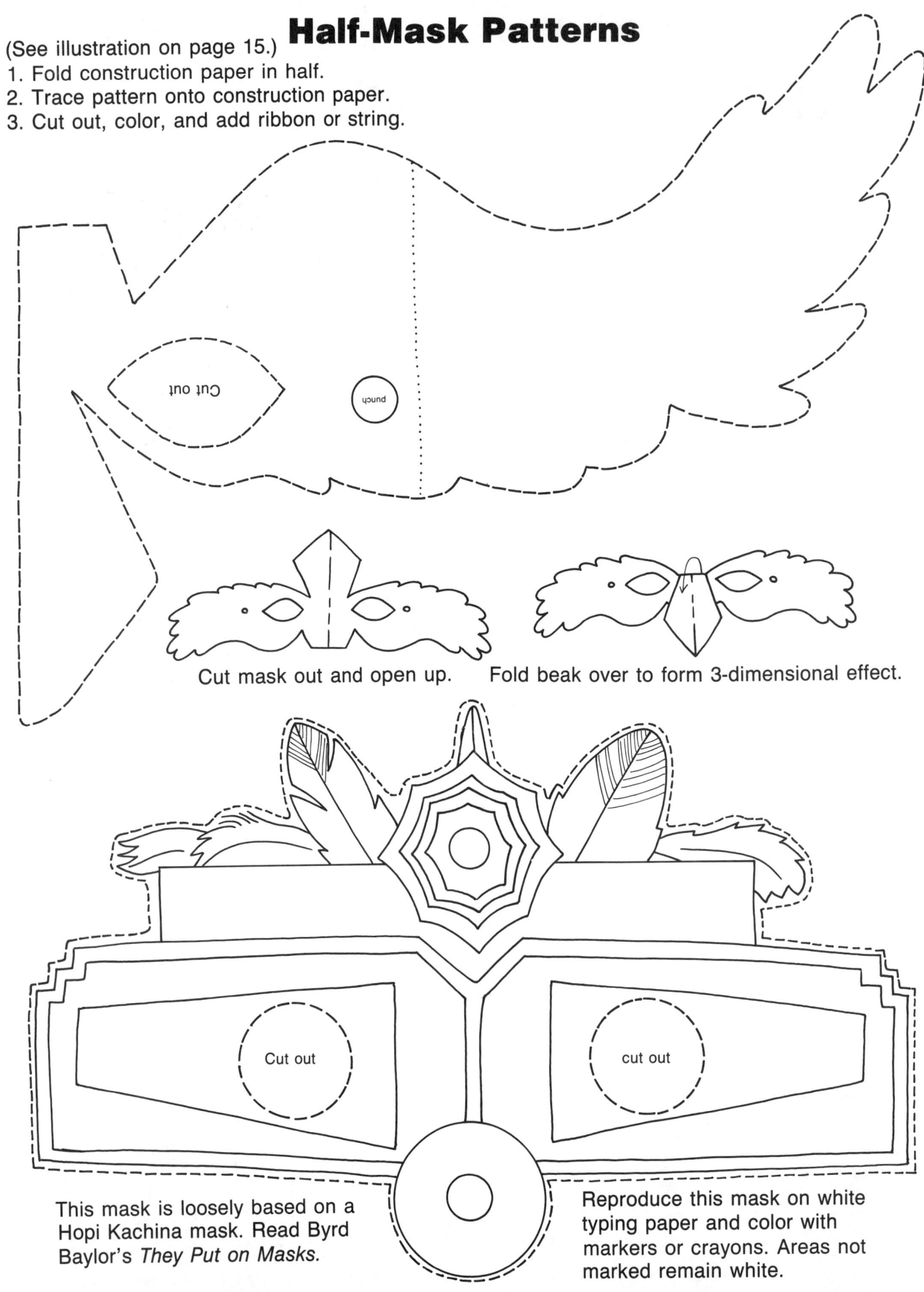

Sculptured Aluminum Foil

The mask as a wall-hanging.

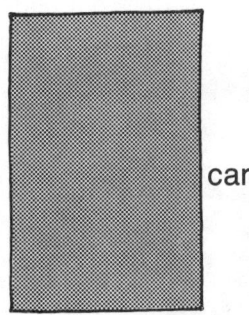

1. Any size will do. An easy-to-work-with size would be 8" x 12".

Tag or cardboard

2. Round the corners.

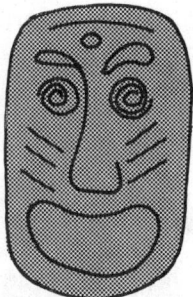

3. Draw the face on the tag with markers

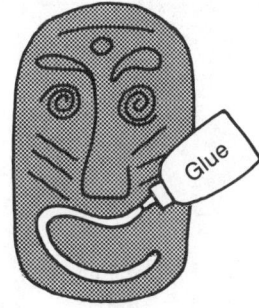

4. Children can follow their own lines with glue. This is the easiest method. Allow glue to dry completely.

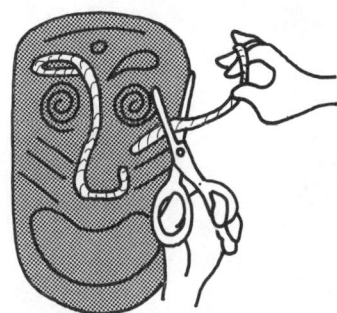

Older children may want to use string.

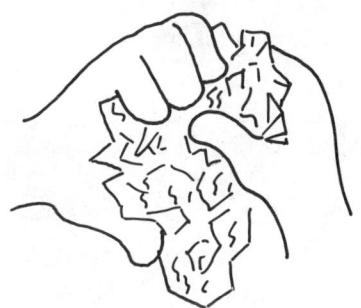

5. Tear off a piece of aluminum foil larger than the mask. Crumple the foil.

6. Smooth out the foil.

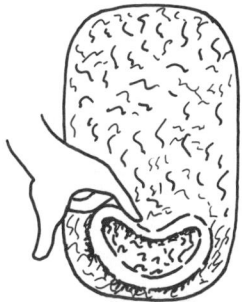

7. Cover mask loosely and press foil in around dried glue design until whole mask face is revealed.

Tell children not to use fingernails or sharp objects because the foil will rip.

8. Press the foil around to the back to clean up the edges.

9. Tape or glue a picture-hanger to the back.

Drinking Straw Mask

The mask as a wall-hanging.

Variations: Consider using a variety of colored straws; cover the background with different colors.

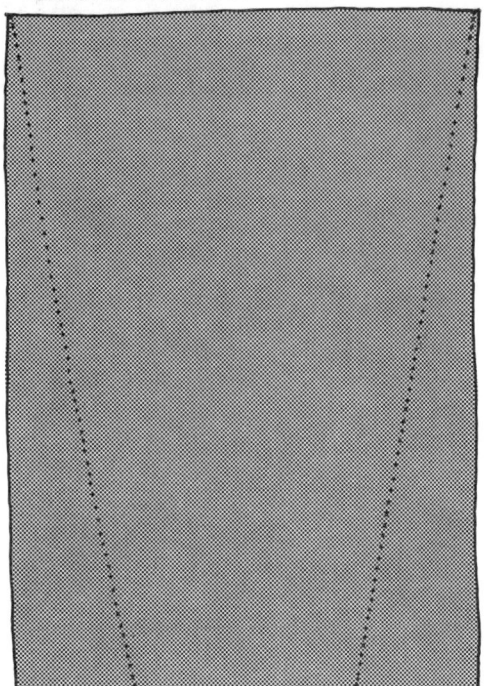

1. Trim tag or cardboard to a very simple shape. Use only straight lines.

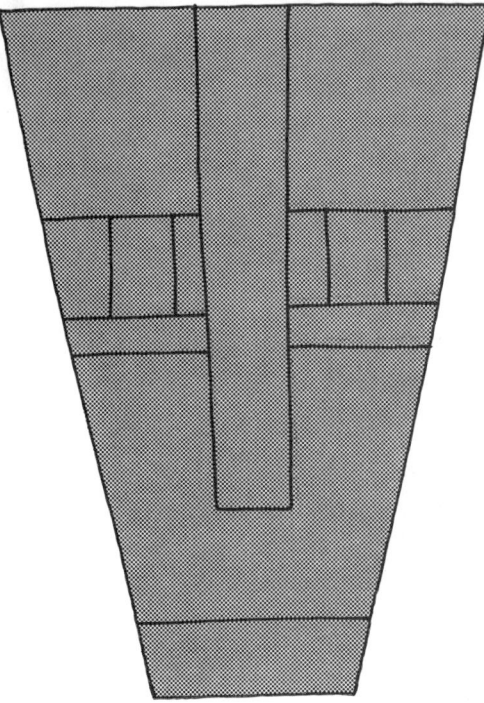

2. Draw your design on the mask. Keep it **very simple**, only straight lines.

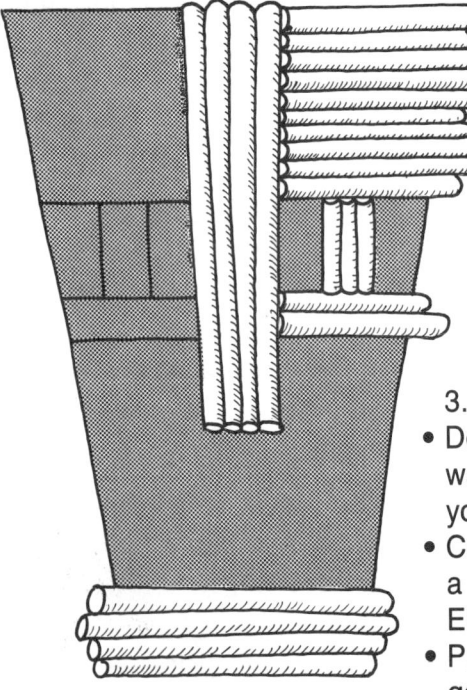

3.
- Decide where you want straws on your design.
- Cover the area with a strong glue like Elmers.
- Press the straws gently into the glue.
- Allow to dry completely before you trim the straws.

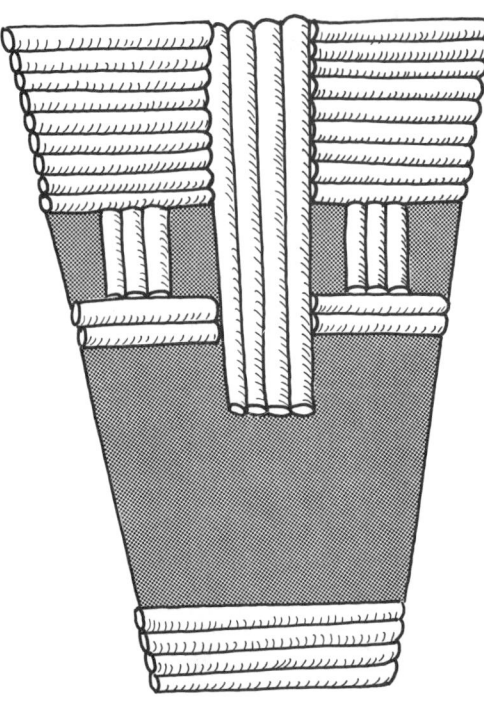

4. Tape or glue a picture hanger to the back.

3-D Bird Beak and Feathers Patterns

Reproduce these pattern pieces for children to color, cut and paste, or make a tag template for children to trace.

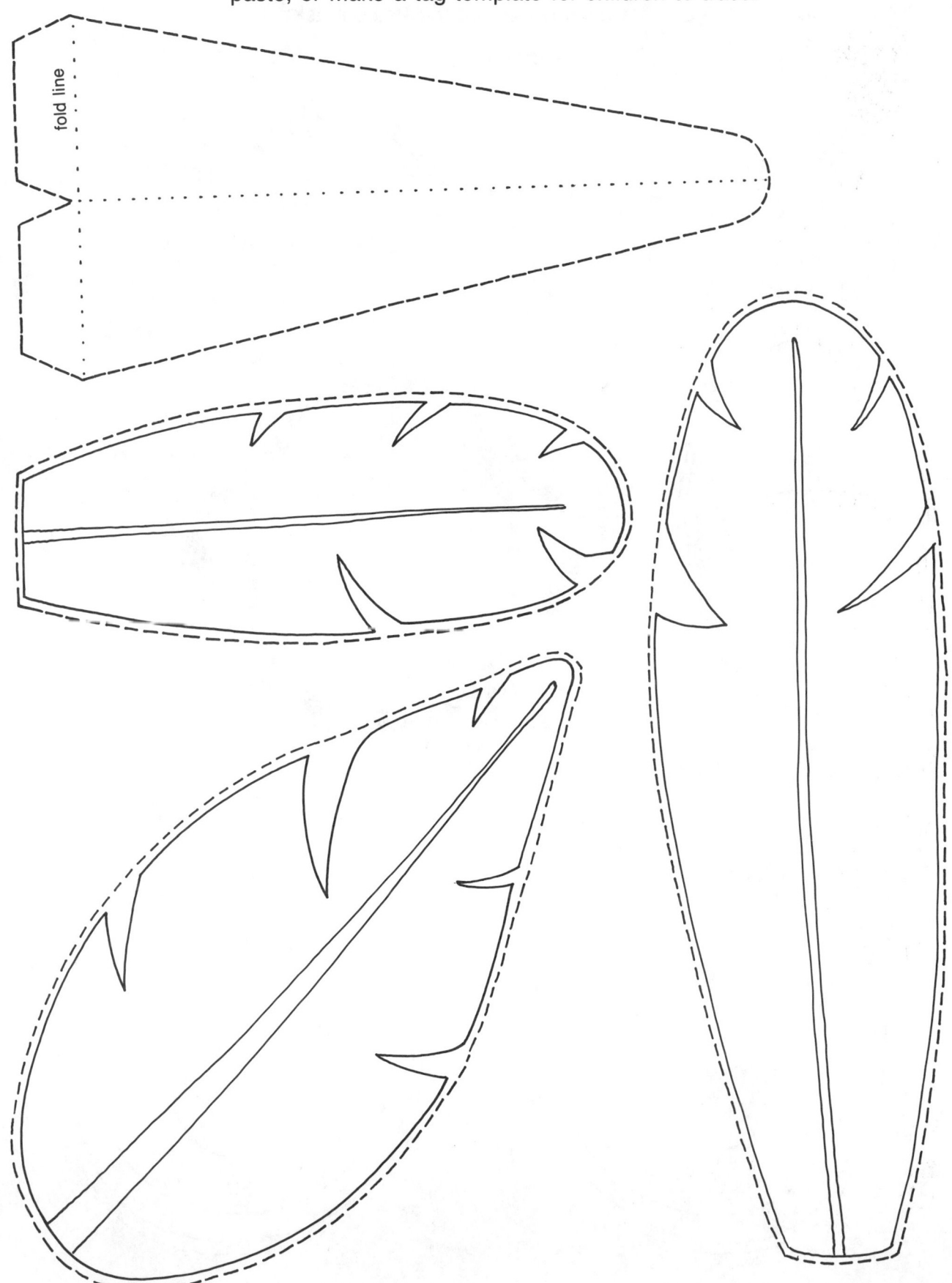

3-D Eyes, Lashes and Brow Patterns

Reproduce on white paper. Color, cut, and glue onto masks. These pattern pieces can be used on any of the basic masks.

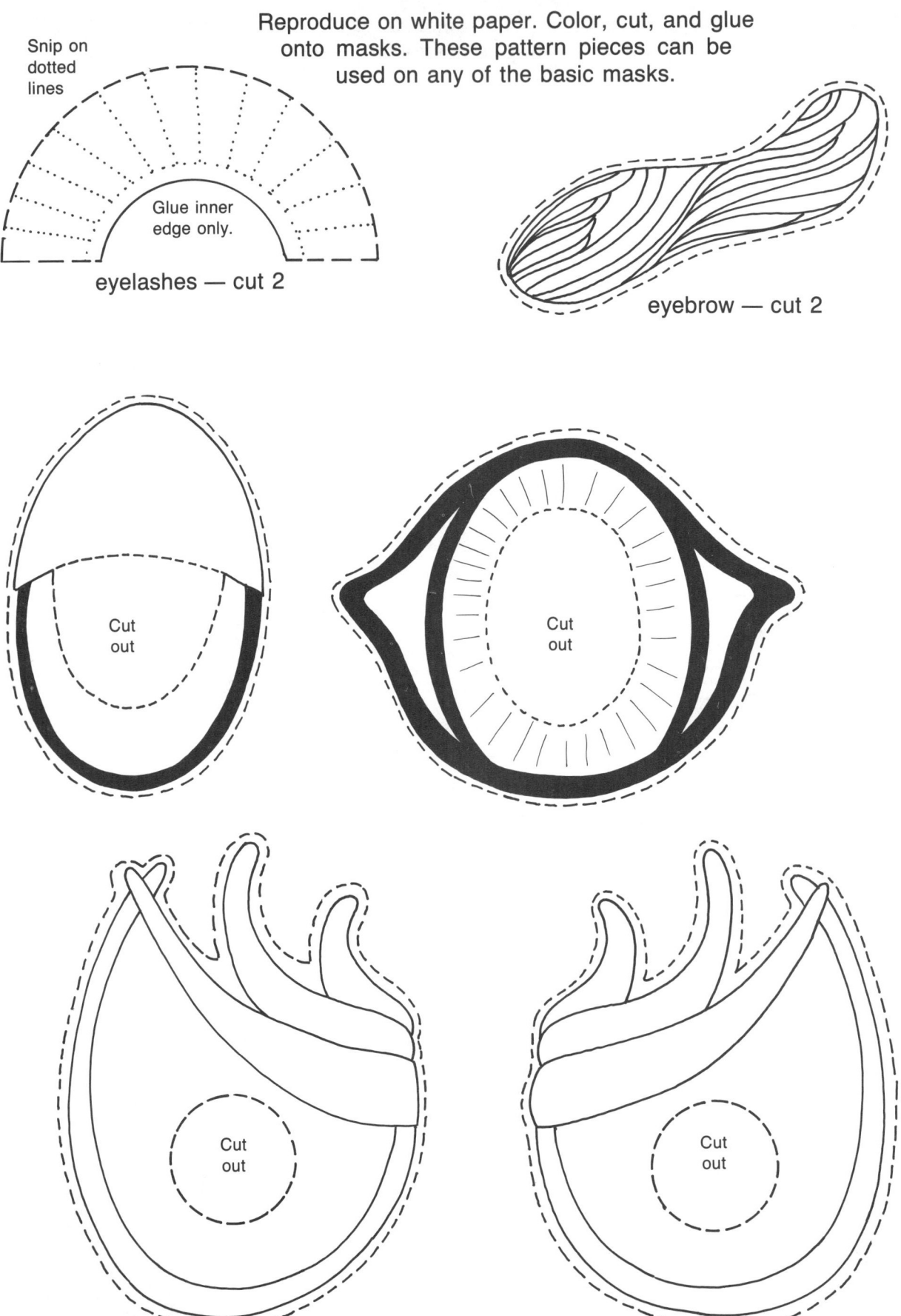

Snip on dotted lines

Glue inner edge only.

eyelashes — cut 2

eyebrow — cut 2

Cut out

© 1988 by EVAN-MOOR CORP. Masks

3-D Mouth Patterns

Reproduce on white paper. Color, cut, and glue onto mask.

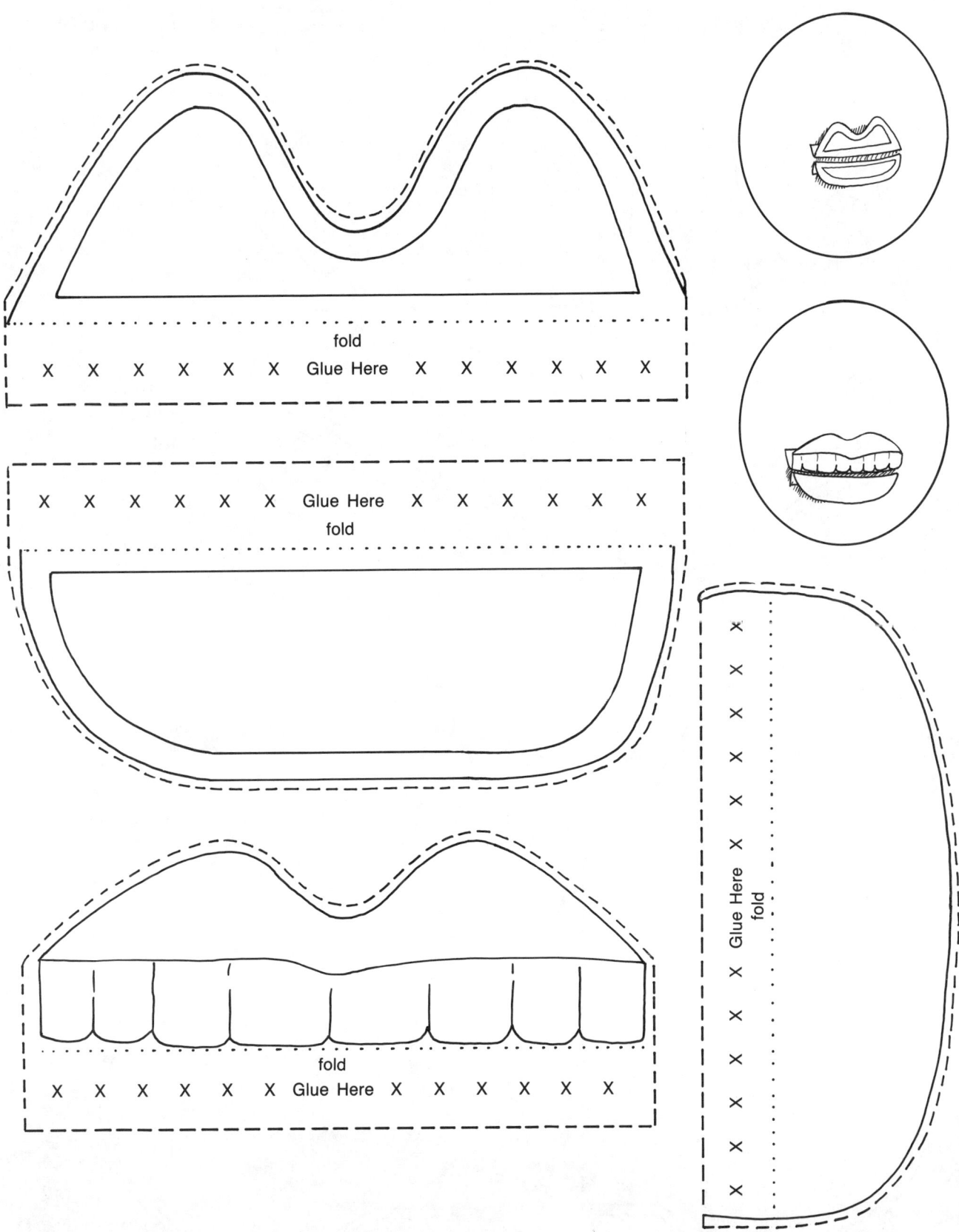

3-D Nose and Ear Patterns

Reproduce on white paper. Color, cut, and glue onto mask.

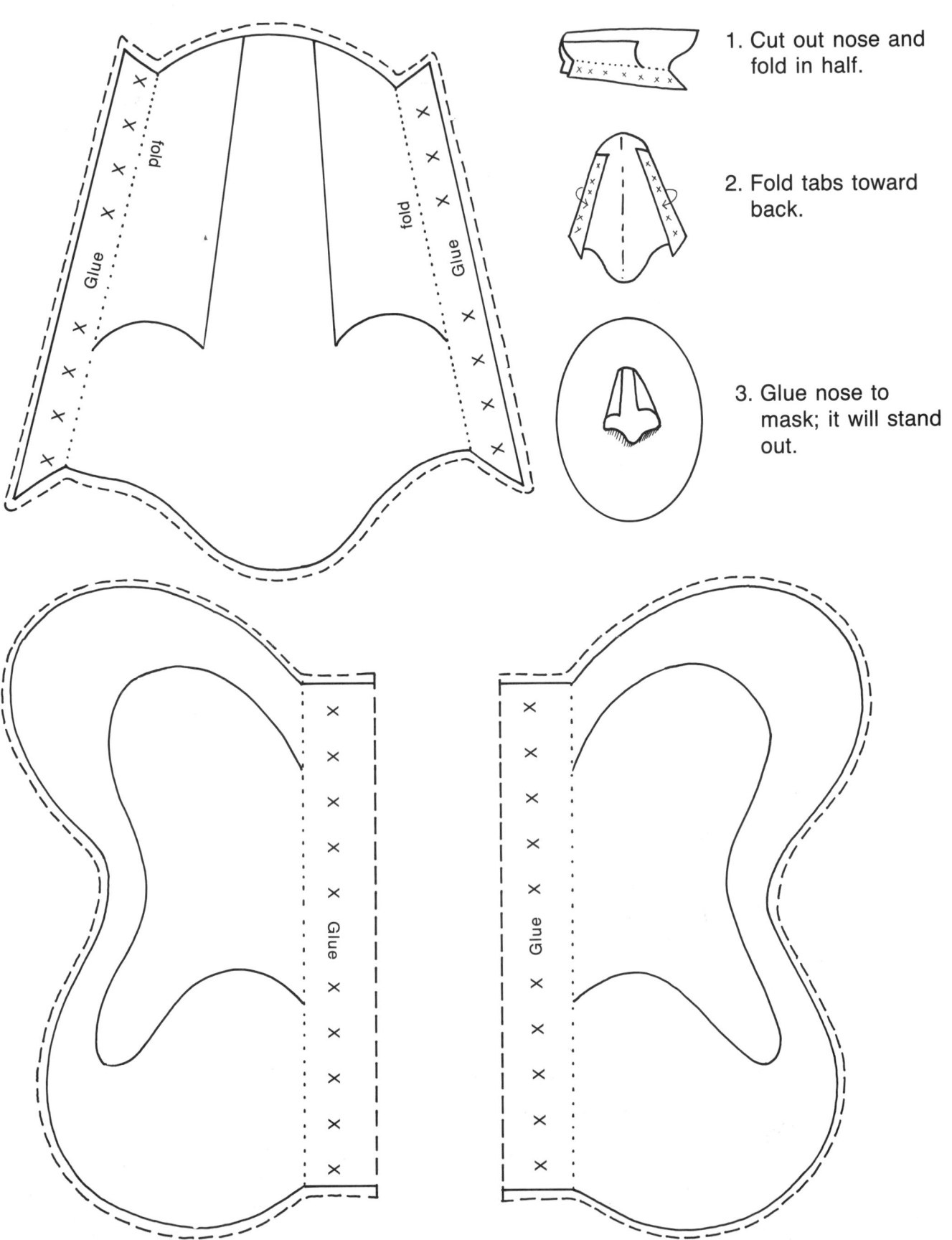

1. Cut out nose and fold in half.
2. Fold tabs toward back.
3. Glue nose to mask; it will stand out.

Clown

A book about masks wouldn't be complete without the clown. The word **mask**, when translated from the Arabic **Masharage** means **clown**.

Carpet

The carpet clown rubs dirt on his face and maybe a little red on his nose, but he lets his skin show. He wears old tattered clothes.

Auguste

This face is known as auguste (pronounced oh-goost). The auguste clown paints his face with colors instead of dirt, but you can still see some of his skin. He is a baggy-pants, slapstick clown.

Whiteface

This is a classic whiteface clown. He covers his face with white greasepaint then uses red and black to paint on a happy or a sad face. He usually wears a skullcap to cover all of his hair. He wears a big ruffle around his neck. There are two types of whiteface: neat and grotesque. Can you tell the difference?

Neat

Grotesque

Eskimo

This nonsymetrical mask is from South West Alaska. Eskimo masks frequently mix up facial features.

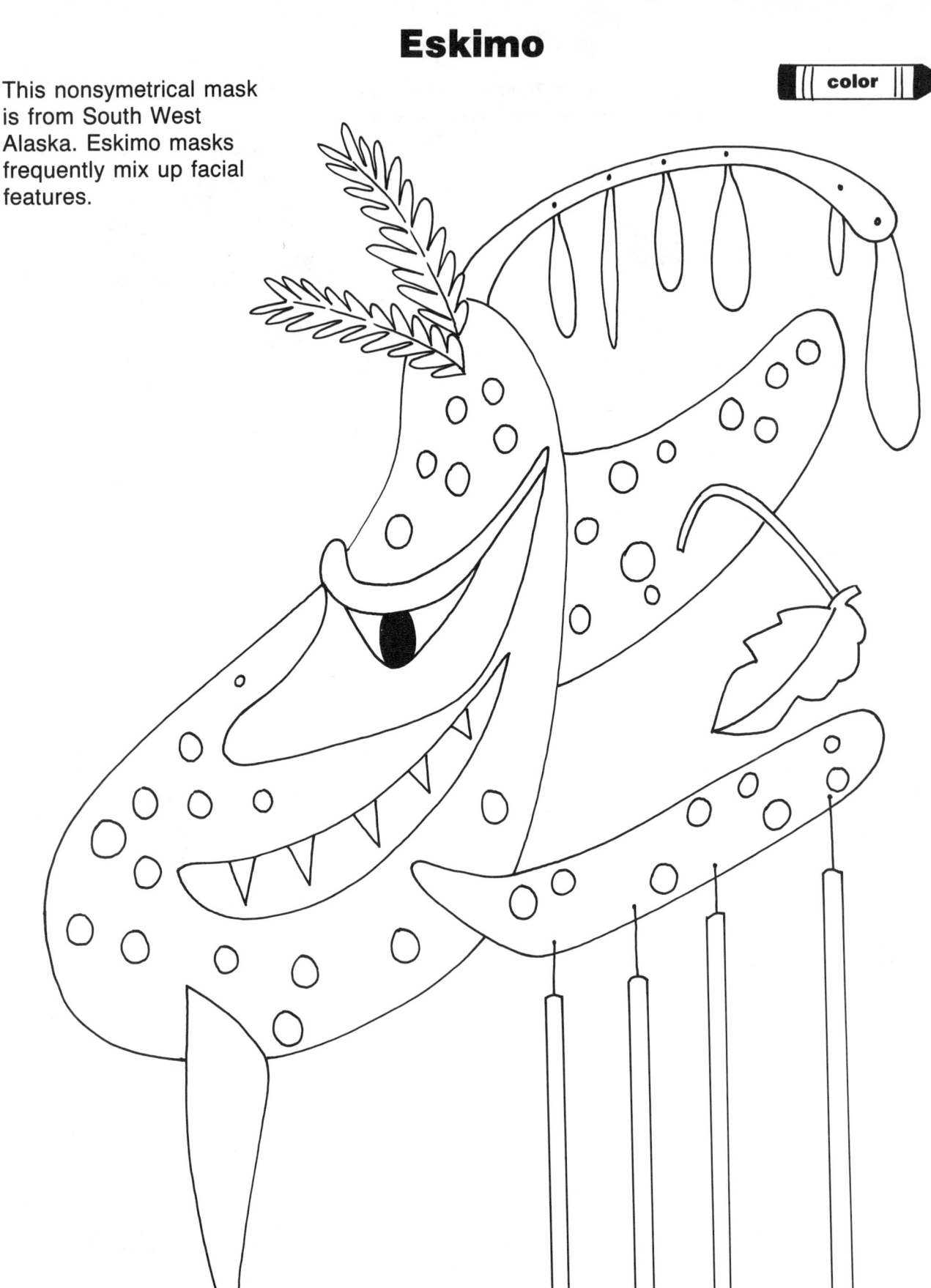

Mexican

color

Yaqui mask — worn by a Pascola dancer from a Piman Tribe, located in Southern Mexico.

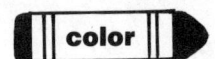

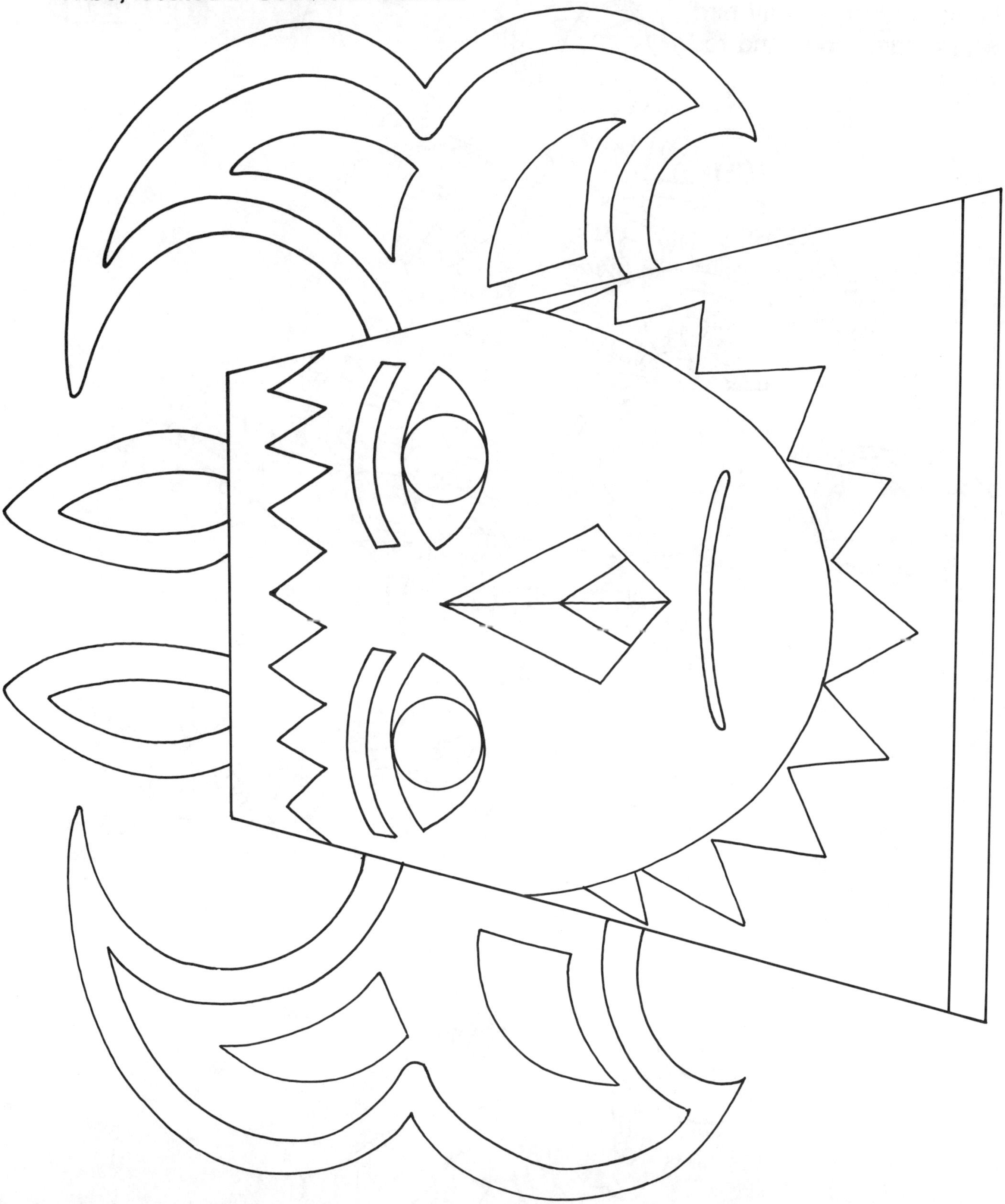

Ceylonese

Garuda — The eagle of Ceylonese myth. A Hindu being, half man, half bird, with golden body and red wings.

American Indian
Kachina

Suggestion:
Begin with a picnic plate and the feather pattern on page 19 to create a 3-dimensional Kachina mask.

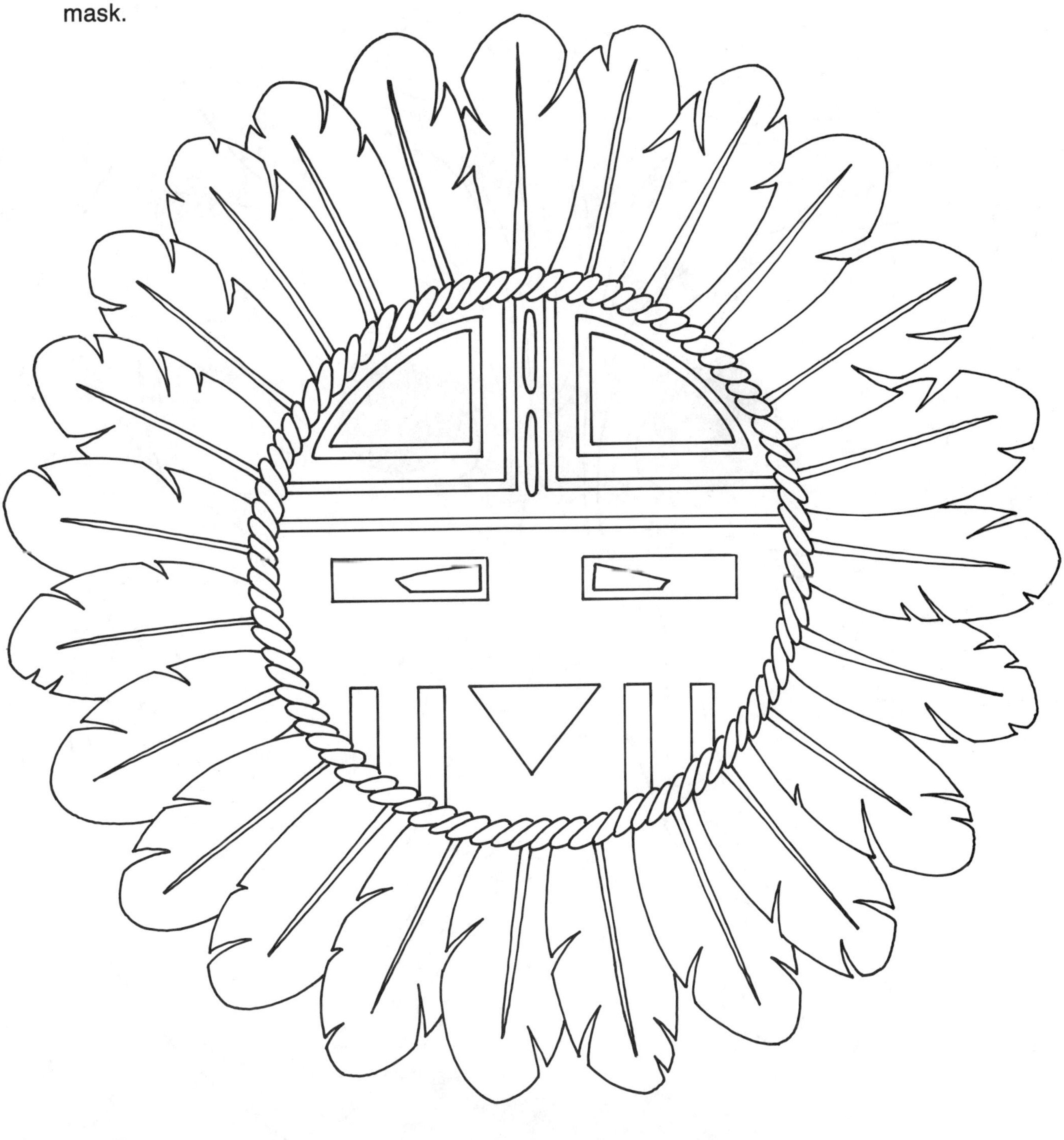

Chinese
Theater Make-Up Mask

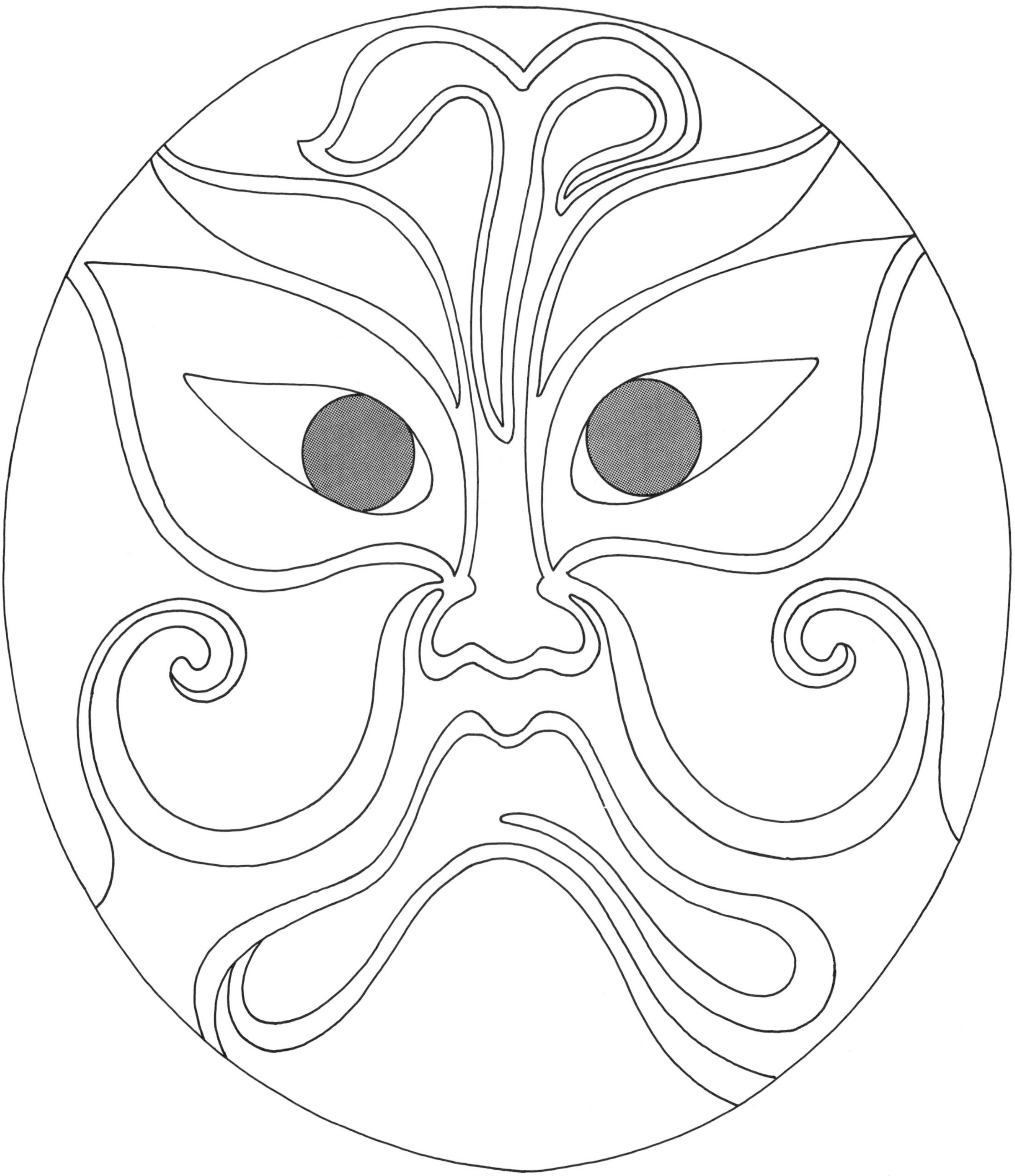

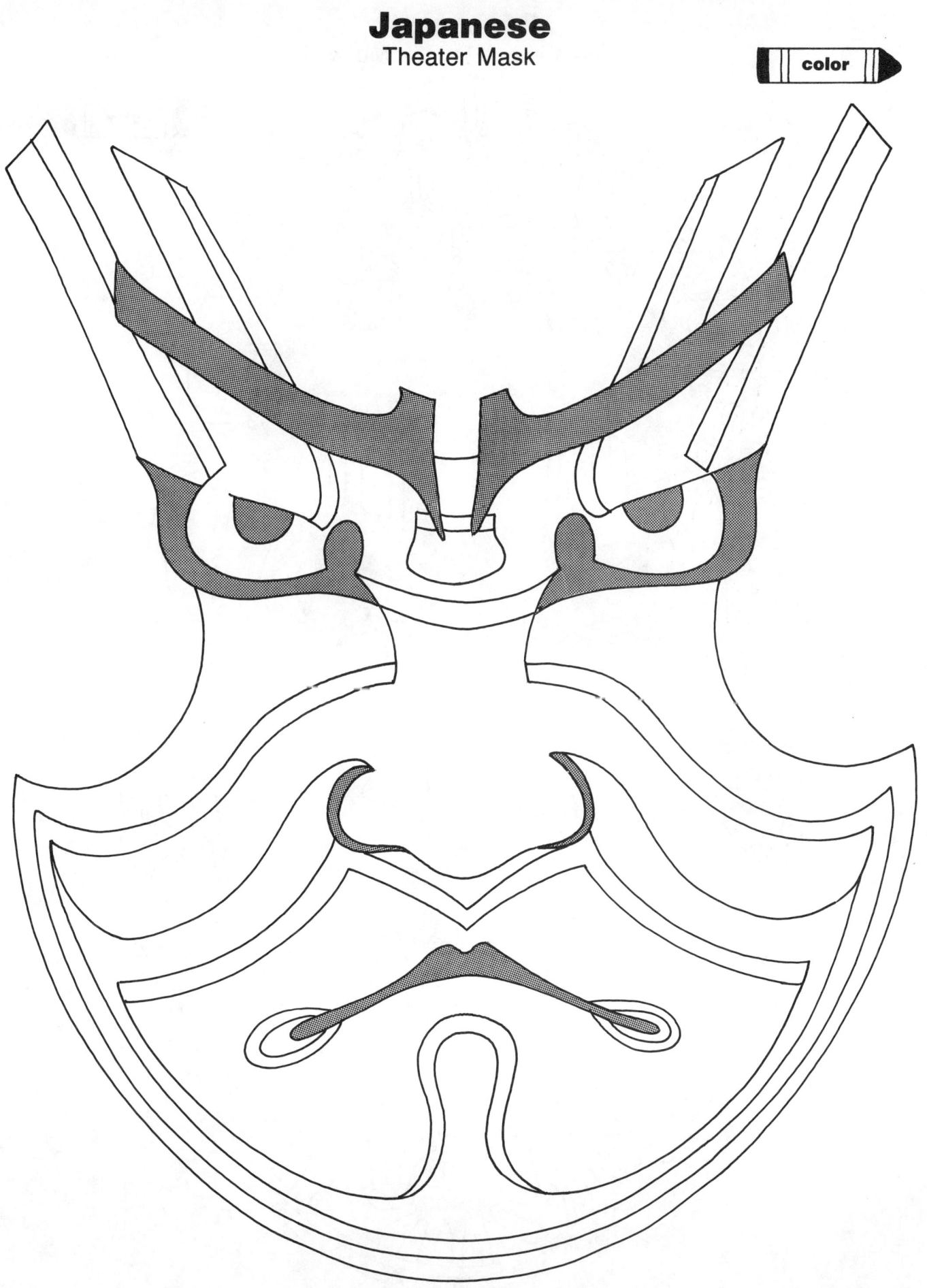

African
Benin Ivory Regalia Mask

Greek
13th-Century Gold Funeral Mask

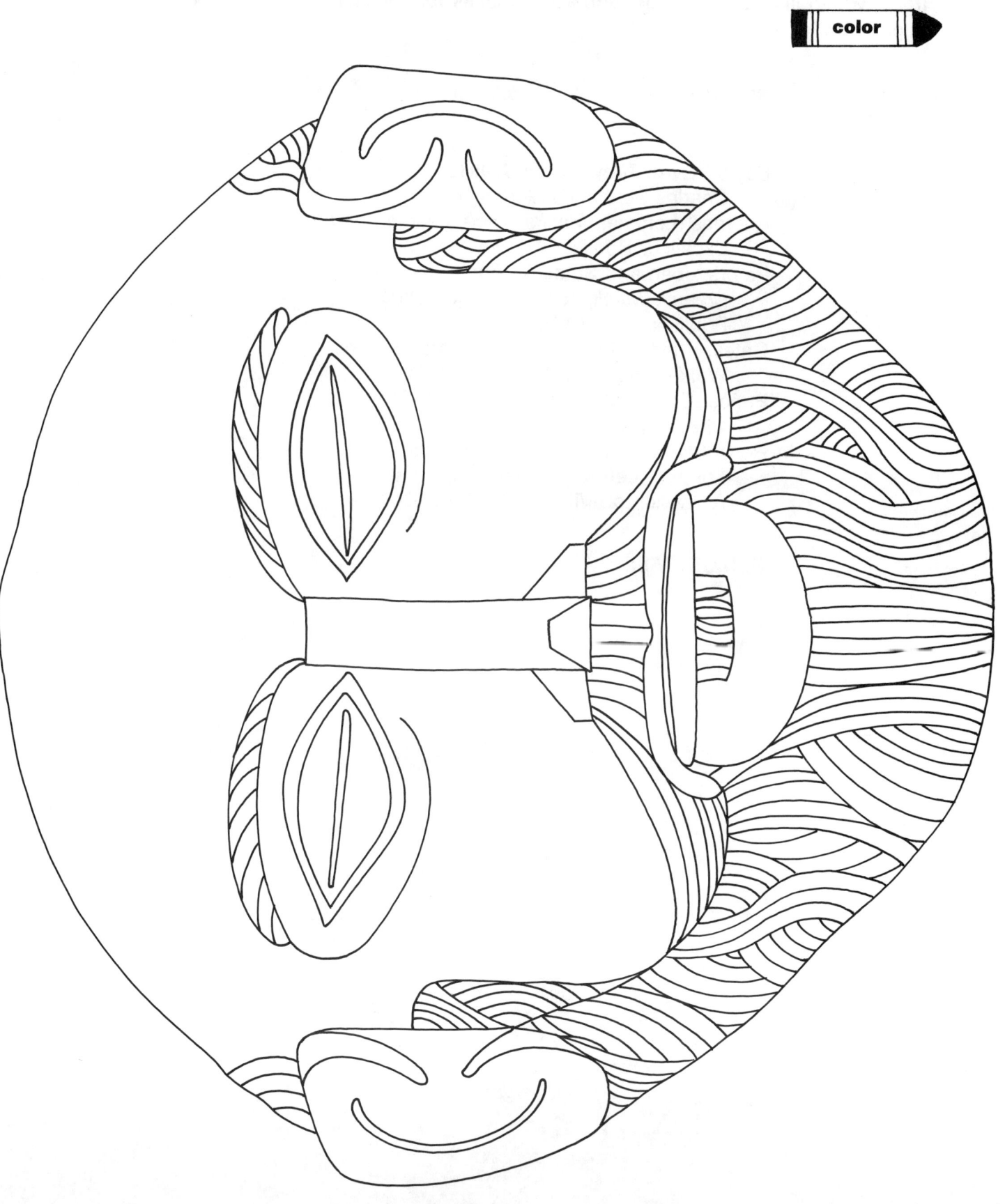

Reading List

If you would like to explore the subject of masks further, here is a list of books you might look for in your library:

BOOKS:

Baylor, Byrd. *They Put On Masks.*
    Charles Scribner's Sons.
Andreas, Lommel. *Masks, Their meaning and function.*
    Excalibur Books.
Peters, Joan and Sutcliffe, Anna.
    Creative Masks for stage and school.
    Publishers, PLAYS, Inc.
Gates, Frieda. *North American Indian Masks.*
    Walker and Company.
Prince, Christine. *Dancing Masks of Africa.*
    Charles Scribner's Sons.
Ross, Laura. *Mask-Making with Pantomime.*
    Lothrop, Lee & Shepard Company
    A division of William Morrow & Company Inc.

PERIODICAL:

Faces, The Magazine About People — Masks
    October, 1987